# New Providence Travel, Rhode Island

Tourism Environment, Vacation, Holiday, Business opportunities

Author
Brian Miller

# Copyright Notice

Copyright © 2017 Global Print Digital
All Rights Reserved

<u>Digital Management Copyright Notice</u>. This Title is not in public domain, it is copyrighted to the original author, and being published by **Global Print Digital**. No other means of reproducing this title is accepted, and none of its content is editable, neither right to commercialize it is accepted, except with the consent of the author or authorized distributor. You must purchase this Title from a vendor who's right is given to sell it, other sources of purchase are not accepted, and accountable for an action against. We are happy that you understood, and being guided by these terms as you proceed. Thank you

First Printing: 2017.

**ISBN:** 978-1-912483-51-8

**Publisher**: Global Print Digital.
Arlington Row, Bibury, Cirencester GL7 5ND
Gloucester
United Kingdom.
Website: www.homeworkoffer.com
.

# Table of Content

Introduction ............................................................... 1
Travel and Tourism ................................................... 5
  *Plan your trip* ........................................................ 18
    Transportation .................................................... 18
    Air Travel ............................................................. 19
    Providence Bus Lines & Charters ....................... 21
    Car Rentals & Limousines .................................. 23
    Public Transportation In .................................... 25
    Rail Service ......................................................... 25
    Weather .............................................................. 27
  *Things to Do in Providence* .................................. 28
    Do in Rhode Island ............................................. 28
      Rhode Island Foods ....................................... 29
      Blackstone Valley .......................................... 31
      Block Island ................................................... 32
      Newport & Bristol County ............................. 34
      South County ................................................ 36
      Warwick ......................................................... 38
    Historic Providence ............................................ 40
      Providence History ....................................... 40
      H.P. Lovecraft ............................................... 44
    Self-Guided Historic Walking Tours ................... 47
      Downtown Historic Tour ............................... 47
      The East Side Historic Walking Tour ............ 49
      The West Side Historic Walking Tour .......... 58
    Providence Performing Arts ............................... 63
      Live Music in Providence .............................. 65
    Arts & Culture ..................................................... 66
    Free Events & Attractions .................................. 69

- Family Fun ........................................................... 72
- Shopping .............................................................. 74
  - Vintage Providence ....................................... 75
- Spas & Salons in The Providence Area ............... 76
- Providence Nightlife ........................................... 77
- LGBT Providence ................................................. 78
- Colleges & Universities ....................................... 79
- Local Sports ........................................................ 84
- Outdoor Adventures ........................................... 87
- Downtown Providence ....................................... 90
- Classes in the Providence Area .......................... 92
- Restaurants ......................................................... 97

*Events ............................................................ 110*
- Annual Events in Providence ............................ 110
- Dining Specials & Events ................................... 116

*Directions & Parking in Providence ..................... 118*

*Tourist Attractions in Providence ........................ 120*

# Introduction

New Providence. One of the oldest cities in the United States, Providence was founded by Roger Williams in 1636 after he was banished from the Massachusetts colony for his religious views.

Born in London around 1603 into a merchant tailor's family, Roger Williams studied law and theology at Cambridge University. As a young minister, his opposition to the established church led him to leave England in 1631 and travel to the new world. He settled in Massachusetts Bay Colony where he continued to challenge the religious order. In the winter of 1635, he was banished from the

Massachusetts Bay Colony for his dissident beliefs. Williams founded Providence on a site at the tip of Narragansett Bay near the Mashassuck River where the farmland was rich and fertile.

By 1643, settlements existed in Providence, Newport, Portsmouth and Warwick. Faced with encroachments from Massachusetts and Connecticut, Williams sailed to England to obtain a charter for the new Rhode Island colony. The charter he received granted independence "comfortable to the laws of England and liberty of the conscience". When efforts were made by other colonies to revoke this charter, Williams returned to England to have it confirmed. King Charles II granted Rhode Island a favorable new charter "to hold forth a lively experiment that a most flourishing civil state may stand and best be maintained with full liberty of religious concernments".

Because of his policy of complete religious toleration, Rhode Island became a haven for refugees from bigotry. Most notable among these were the Quakers from Boston. In 1680, a wharf was built to facilitate trade and Providence's days of prosperity began. As a port in the 1700's, fortunes were made in shipbuilding, whaling, trade with China and the thriving triangle of trade in Molasses, Rum and Slaves.

When the British occupied Newport during the Revolutionary War, many Newport merchants fled to Providence and established themselves in trade there. Foremost among them was the Brown family that brought wealth and fame to the city. John Brown, a merchant and shipbuilder, opened trade with China. Joseph, an architect, designed many of the city's finest buildings. Nicholas donated land and money to establish the university that bears the family name. Moses began the American industrial revolution by financing the first water powered spinning mill built by Samuel Slater.

Today, Providence is the largest city in Rhode Island and the third largest in New England after Boston and Worcester. It is among the region's leaders in the production of machinery, jewelry and silver and is a major port and financial center

# Travel and Tourism

## Providence, Rhode Island: New England's coolest city

With experimental arts, foodie culture and spectacular displays, Providence has huge charm. Pamela Petro offers an in-depth guide

Providence, Rhode Island, is the coolest city in New England. I would even put it on the shortlist of coolest small cities in the United States. (It has about 170,000 people, with another million in the surrounding area.)

Like Rome, Providence congregates around seven hills. The two to keep in mind are Federal and College. Like many cities, it's traversed by a river; unlike most, its river had been paved over by the world's widest concrete bridge until the Nineties, when it was uncovered and brilliantly lit a fire. More on that later.

Like few other cities, Providence gives tax incentives to artists not institutions. And unlike any other, it was founded by Roger Williams, one of the great iconoclasts of the 17th century. Williams was kicked out of Massachusetts Bay for daring to believe in religious freedom and the separation of church and state. He founded Providence as a haven of tolerance.

Williams said, "When you do what you do best, you are not only helping yourself but the world." What Providence does best today is create: art, food, architecture and faculties for critical thought, to name a few of its strengths. It is home to Brown University the hippest Ivy League school, founded by an 18th-century slave trader, once home to Emma Watson (of Harry Potter fame) as well as six other colleges and universities including Rhode Island School of Design, perennially the number one art school in the US.

RISD (pronounced "Rizdee") is responsible not only for the city's vibrant, experimental arts scene the downtown and jewellery districts are packed with galleries and studios but for making Providence the foodie capital of New England. Chefs such as Bruce Tillinghast, of New Rivers restaurant, began in the visual but veered into the culinary arts. Tillinghast says, "I find both colour and food very sensual. The creative leap you make when you imagine colour in your head is the same as when you imagine flavour: one employs vision and the other taste."

Brown and RISD cling to College Hill (well, RISD clings to the slope; Brown crowns the crest) on Providence's smart East Side, which is home to some of the America's most magnificent early architecture. In fact there are more intact colonial homes in Providence than anywhere else in the US.

The place to see them is Benefit Street, once a red-light district so down on its luck that no one could afford to bulldoze the dilapidated old buildings in hindsight, a stroke of luck. Today it's a showcase of 200 years of American architecture, from clapboard colonials to gabled and turreted Victorians.

To get a sense of the city's diversity ethnically, geographically, historically head down College Hill (carefully; it's steep, and the pavements are of uneven brick) to Waterplace Park, a resurrected cove that was also once hidden under concrete.

Like the Riverwalk that blends into it, Waterplace Park is the site of art festivals and concert series in summer, and ice skating in winter. Its greatest triumph is a sculpture installation called WaterFire: on selected nights throughout the year, volunteers in rowing boats stoke wood into wrought-iron urns anchored in the river, and set the logs blazing.

There's nothing like it anywhere else in the world. The medieval smell of wood smoke in a contemporary urban setting, and the elemental play of water and fire stir an uncanny pairing of opposites guaranteed to raise hairs on the back of your neck.

From downtown head up to Federal Hill, the increasingly sophisticated Little Italy (once the mob capital of New England), filled with Italian cafés, restaurants and stores. The centre line of Atwells Avenue, the main street, is painted the shades of the Italian flag: red, white and green.

You might be glad of a hat on this walk. The wind whips off Narragansett Bay the sea whipped in once, too, during the 1938 hurricane, and inundated downtown. You can often smell the ocean, and its promise of wide-open horizons, in the heart of the city. Which is one more of Providence's charms. Tiny Rhode Island has almost 3,500 miles of sandy beaches, and its capital is no more than an hour from any and just one hour from Boston and Cape Cod, and three from New York.

**Getting there**
British Airways (www.ba.com) flies to Boston for £450 return; from Boston, the MBTA Commuter Rail to Providence costs £6.50 and takes just over an hour. Or fly Continental Airlines (www.continental.com) to Providence's T F Green Airport via Newark (the easiest-navigated of all NYC-area airports), for £380 return.

**Staying there**
Providence has its share of competent chain hotels the Westin and Hilton plus a hoary favourite, the Biltmore. Here are some excellent independent options.

Hotel Providence (001 44 401 861 8000; www.hotelprovidence.com) is the city's premier boutique hotel. In the heart of downtown, it's serious about attending to travelers' needs fine bedding, concierge service, Wi-Fi, fitness studio but is also intimate and eclectic. Rooms are stylistically inspired by authors such as Tolstoy, Dumas, Alcott and Dickinson. Its restaurant, Aspire, and bar, A-bar, are two of the hottest venues in town. Doubles from £145 to £463.

Hotel Dolce Villa (401 383 7031; www.dolcevillari.com) is one of a few lodging options in Little Italy, on Federal Hill. It's a suite hotel (nine one-bedrooms, five two-bedrooms); all suites have kitchens, which makes this a good option for a money-saving, multiple-night stay. A snappy white-on-white scheme runs throughout. Doubles from £107 to £196.

The Old Court Bed & Breakfast (401 751 2002; www.oldcourt.com) is a converted rectory on fabled Benefit Street a great location for exploring College Hill or downtown. Beautifully appointed inside and out, its antique-filled rooms manage to be elegant and comfortable. Breakfasts are home-made. Ten double rooms range from £73 to £130.

**Eating & drinking**
Intimate and freshly renovated, in an old College Hill building, New Rivers (401 751 0350; www.newriversrestaurant.com) is one of the city's best bets. Dishes made from local, organic ingredients feature native cod, Vermont quail and creative pastas. Prix fixe menu at £17.

One of the standouts on Federal Hill is Mediterraneo Caffe (401 331 7760; www.mediterraneocaffe.com). A favourite among visiting celebrities (Cameron Diaz and Alec Baldwin were spotted there recently), it has a great wine list and hip atmosphere. The Italian fare is authentic with a stylish touch. Dinner for two with wine costs about £64.

For lighter meals don't miss Olga's Cup and Saucer (401 831 6666; http://olgascup andsaucer.blogspot.com/), an artisanal bakery and café owned by another RISD graduate that is open for breakfast and lunch in the arty jewellery district, and Andreas (401 331 7879; www.andreasri.com), a long-time Greek-flavoured favourite on Thayer Street, in the heart of the Brown campus.

For good booze and a relaxed pub atmosphere, try Finnegan's Draft House (401 751 0290) downtown, which consistently draws a crowd for its huge selection of beers and perfectly cooked food.

If you have a car, drive to East Providence for authentic Portuguese food (Portuguese-speaking communities have thrived in southern New England since 19th-century whaling days). Try the octopus at the reasonable Estrela Do Mar (401 434 5621).

I'm putting this next item in with "Drink" and as a segue to art. Lupo's Heartbreak Hotel (401 272 5876; www.lupos.com) has been the go-to club since I was a student in Providence, circa 1980. It books everyone from new bands to big names looking for an intimate space, and is the best live music venue in town. Cover charges range from £8 to £24.

**Art notes**
Don't miss one of the WaterFire river installations: see www.waterfire.org for times and dates, and plan your visit accordingly.

Because it's a teaching museum, the RISD Museum (401 454 8500; www.risdmuseum.org) has a comprehensive collection, from ancient to ultra-contemporary artefacts, and is one of the great small museums in the US. Check out the costume and textile holdings.

Another must is RISD Works (401 277 4949; www.risdworks.com), which sells fine and applied art by RISD graduates. Some of the work is mind-blowing.

AS220 (401 861 9190; www.as220.org) is a uniquely Providence venture, vital to both working artists and their audiences. It has gallery space, a darkroom, print shop, studios, performance space and a good bar (its sangria gets high marks), and serves vegetarian-friendly food. Go to create, see, eat, drink and listen preferably not all at once.

Check out Providence's Gallery Night (www.gallerynight.info), which happens the third Thursday of every month, from March until November. Art buses cruise around to the city's galleries including Gallery 17 Peck (401 331 2561; www.17peck.com), a force in contemporary art, photography, and American Indian art. Free themed, bike, and walking tours.

The Providence Art Club (401 331 1114; www.providenceartclub.org) occupies nearly a whole block of Thomas Street one of the steepest roads leading up College Hill. It offers artists studio and gallery space in a collection of clapboard and brick buildings, and one half-timbered, craftsman-style extravaganza. Worth a look for the outside, as well as what's on show inside.

## Other things to do

You can saunter down Benefit Street on your own and mosey into the Brown campus University Hall was a Revolutionary War barracks (the soldiers stole all the brass doorknobs) but it's far more interesting to walk with a Rhode Island Historical Society guide (401 273 7507, ext 62; www.rihs.org). Walk-in tours run from June 15 to October 15 and cost £7. For £10 you can also tour the John Brown House Museum (built in 1786 by the man who founded Brown University).

Some concluding advice: when the wind gets to you, go to the movies at the Cable Car (401 272 3970; www.cablecarcinema.com), a cinema/café with sofa seating, or the Art Deco Avon Cinema (401 421 3315; www.avoncinema.com), at the bottom and top of College Hill, respectively. Both show art house fare. Or if you have a yen to shop, hit Thayer Street before the Avon movie; it bisects Brown's campus and attracts hip, college-age types. Wickenden Street, in the still Portuguese-flavoured Fox Point neighbourhood, abutting Brown, has funkier options. Or just give in and go downtown to Providence Place (401 270 1000; www.providenceplace.com), probably the best mall in New England.

Just to say you did it: drop in on Ladd Observatory on College Hill (401 863 2323; www.brown.edu/ Departments /Physics / Ladd ), a tiny structure built in 1891 that offers free telescope-viewing every Tuesday night. Or visit the Culinary Museum of Johnson & Wales (401 598 2805; www.culinary.org), which hordes menus and cookbooks going back to the 16th century, Chinese and Egyptian artefacts, and even an authentic American diner from 1925. Admission £4.

# Plan your trip

## Transportation

Rhode Island is easy to reach by air, rail or highway. Warwick's T.F. Green Airport is just 10 minutes from Providence, and Amtrak and MBTA rail service is located in the heart of downtown. Once here, Providence and Warwick offer ample car rental, limousine and charter bus options. The Rhode Island Public Transit Authority (known as RIPTA) provides convenient public bus transportation throughout the state.

## Air Travel

For those flying into Rhode Island, Warwick's Green International Airport (PVD) is only 10 minutes from downtown Providence, and is conveniently located right off of Interstate 95. A favorite of business and leisure travelers, Green was named the third best airport in the U.S., as well as best in New England in the *Condé Nast Traveler* 2015 Readers' Choice Awards.

Green International Airport is easily accessible to Boston, Cape Cod and Southeastern New England. Green is a popular alternative to Boston's Logan Airport and offers seamless transportation connections with direct access to MBTA train service.

Green offers more than 100 flights daily via major carriers, including:

Allegiant Airlines 702-505-8888
American Airlines 800-433-7300

Azores Airlines 508-677-0555

Delta Air Lines 800-221-1212

Frontier Airlines 801-401-9000

JetBlue 800-538-2583

New England Airlines 800-243-2460

Norwegian Airlines 800-357-4159

OneJet 844-663-5381

Southwest Airlines 800-435-9792

TACV Cabo Verde Airlines 866-359-8228

United Airlines 800-241-6522

InterLink at Green Airport

Green's eco-friendly InterLink hub provides passengers with an array of transportation options. Conveniently housing a rental car facility, public transportation options, and rail service to Providence, Boston and beyond, the InterLink offers travelers ease, affordability and accessibility.

## International Travelers

Boston's Logan International Airport features nonstop air service from more than 100 worldwide destinations. Located less than 50 miles from Providence, Logan offers convenient transportation options from Boston, including bus service pickup within steps of all five if its airport terminals. Peter Pan's 10 daily departures leave directly from Logan to downtown Providence, and Amtrak and commuter rail service is readily available from Boston

# Providence Bus Lines & Charters

An ideal hub-and-spoke destination, many bus and charter services offer transportation from Providence to points throughout the Northeast.

## Academy Express, Llc.

Since its inception in 1968, Academy Bus has been committed to raising the standards of ground transportation. This is why Academy Bus is the largest privately owned transportation company in the United States, with the most modern bus charter fleet on the East Coast. Our top priorities are customer service and well-maintained vehicles that are customized to our clients' needs. In addition to providing exceptional service to private parties all across the Northeast, Academy services a number of Professional and Collegiate Athletic Teams. Academy currently operates four different sized vehicles, with capacities of 15, 30, 38, and 54; Academy can get you to where you need to be

## All Occasion Transportation, Inc.

All Occasion Transportation offers service locally and in over 600 cities WORLDwide, with sedans, premium sedans, limousines, luxury SUV's, executive vans, Mercedes Sprinters, Executive Trolleys, 29 & 31 passenger Minicoaches, Motorcoaches and the area's only Mercedes S Class and Audi A8 service. All Occasion

Transportation is proud to be named "Best Limousine Company in America."

### Viking Tours
Viking Tours operates a fleet of motorcoaches, minicoaches and old-fashioned trolleys available for touring and transportation throughout Rhode Island. We also provide guide and receptive services for groups wishing to tour the Rhode Island area.

## Car Rentals & Limousines

Looking for a luxurious ride or a last-minute ride up town? Providence has limo and taxi services to suit your needs.

### All Occasion Transportation, Inc.
All Occasion Transportation offers service locally and in over 600 cities WORLDwide, with sedans, premium sedans, limousines, luxury SUV's, executive vans, Mercedes Sprinters, Executive Trolleys, 29 & 31

passenger Minicoaches, Motorcoaches and the area's only Mercedes S Class and Audi A8 service. All Occasion Transportation is proud to be named "Best Limousine Company in America."

## Arrow Prestige Limo

Arrow Prestige Limousine & Coach is Rhode Island's premier transportation company. Our fleet consists of Mercedes Benz and Lincoln Town Car Sedans, Sport Utility Vehicles, Limousines, Passenger Vans, Executive Shuttles and Luxury Coaches. You can see all our vehicles at www.arrowprestigelimo.com

## Enterprise Rent-A-Car

Need a rental? We'll pick you up! Rent from one of several RI and SE MA locations, including the Providence Airport and Downtown Providence location, located on the first floor of the RI Convention Center

## Zipcar

Zipcar is a member based car sharing service with cars located locally in Providence, Bristol and Newport. Reservations by the hour or the day with gas and insurance included.

## Public Transportation In

The Rhode Island Public Transit Authority (RIPTA) offers low-cost bus service throughout Rhode Island.

Visitors to Providence can access the city's Downtown, Federal Hill and East Side neighborhoods through RIPTA's Providence LINK Trolley. LINK trolleys run on CNG (compressed natural gas), a clean fuel, and offer two routes to Providence's restaurants, hotels, theaters, universities, historic sites, shopping and more. The cost is $2 per person, per ride or $6 for a one-day pass.

## Rail Service

**Amtrak**
Providence is conveniently located on Amtrak's Northeast Corridor route, which runs from Boston to Washington, D.C. and back. High-speed Acela service easily transports passengers from New York City to Providence in about two hours and 30 minutes. The train station is located at 100 Gaspee Street, in the heart of the downtown area. For tickets call 1-800-USA-RAIL or visit www.amtrak.com.

Amtrak offers some discounted fares on regional service. For special rates, visit www.Amtrak.com / VisitRI.

**MBTA**
The Massachusetts Bay Transportation Authority (MBTA) runs low-cost, round-trip rail service from Boston to downtown Providence and to Warwick's T.F. Green Airport. Complete schedule and pricing information for the Providence-Stoughton route may

be found at www.MBTA.com or by calling 1-800-392-6100.

During football season, the MBTA also runs service from Green Airport and Providence to Gillette Stadium. Check the www.MBTA.com during the season for more information.

## Weather

Providence, Rhode Island's average temperature for the entire year is nearly 50 degrees, with April through June, and September through mid-November being the most delightfully moderate seasons. January and February are the coldest months, with a mean temperature near 29 degrees, and July and August are the warmest, with a mean close to 72 degrees.

Providence, RI's weather has no regular "rainy" or "dry" season, with precipitation fairly evenly distributed throughout the year. The first measurable snowfall of winter generally comes toward the end of November, but may be as late as January. The month with the heaviest snowfall is typically February.

## Providence Weather - Clothing Index

### Winter
Layer clothing, and be sure to pack long-sleeved shirts, sweaters, socks, a medium-to-heavy coat, and gloves.

### Spring & Fall
Bring long-sleeved shirts or light sweaters, raincoats, an umbrella and a light jacket.

### Summer
Pack lightly, with shorts, t-shirts, sandals, a windbreaker or light sweater for evening, and - of course - your bathing suit.

# Things to Do in Providence
Do in Rhode Island

## Rhode Island Foods

For a small place, Rhode Island is jam-packed with culinary traditions. Like the state itself, our signature foods are quirky, fun and sure to please.

One of the easiest ways to pinpoint a native Rhode Islander is to have them say this word: "quahog." A type of hard-shelled clam, the quahog is Rhode Island's unofficial mascot. Unlike our tight-jawed brethren to the north, who pronounce it "ko-hog," Rhode Islanders say "kwah-hog." No matter how you say it, quahogs are delicious in a variety of ways: shucked and served straight from the sea, added to red sauce and served over spaghetti, or chopped, mixed with stuffing and put back into the half shell - affectionately known as the "stuffie."

Providence is the birthplace of the diner, dating back to 1872. The most beloved of all local diners is Haven Brothers, a trailer on wheels that parks nightly next to

Providence City Hall. From blue collars to bluebloods, everyone stops at Haven Brothers, which serves burgers and other treats from the grill until the wee small hours. Another local tradition is Olneyville New York System, which has been serving their signature wieners since the 1930s. Those in the know order them "all the way," which means slathered in onions, mustard, celery salt and their top secret spicy meat sauce.

How do you wash down these delicious delicacies? With one of two of Rhode Island's favorite beverages. Del's Lemonade is the taste of summer sunshine. Based on a classic Neopolitan recipe, the frozen, sweet/tart beverage features real hunks of lemon. Long before coffee became trendy, Rhode Islanders were crazy for coffee milk. In fact, it has been named the official state beverage of Rhode Island. Similar to chocolate milk, milk is mixed with a coffee-flavored syrup. There are two different types of coffee syrup - Autocrat and Eclipse. Both have die-hard devotees.

## Blackstone Valley

Northern Rhode Island is home to Blackstone Valley, the birthplace of the Industrial Revolution. Blackstone Valley's historical roots combined with ample arts offerings and festivals, unique restaurants, and varied attractions make it an ideal spot for a wide range of visitors.

Immerse yourself in history at one of Blackstone Valley's museums and historic sites, including Slater Mill, a National Historic Landmark. Take in a Pawtucket Red Soxgame, Boston's AAA baseball team, or head to Twin River Casino, the state's largest gaming and entertainment venue. Tour the area by water on the Blackstone River Explorer, with rides offered throughout much of the spring, summer and fall. Or spend a unique overnight on the Samuel Slater Canal Boat, the state's only floating bed and breakfast.

Outdoor enthusiasts will find many options for canoeing, kayaking, fishing and biking. Hikers and campers can explore the many parks, management areas and campgrounds in Blackstone Valley. And for those looking for a hands-on experience, visit some of the many farms in the region where you can pick your own apples, pumpkins, berries and more. Come winter, hop aboard The Polar ExpressTM Train Ride, an ever-popular attraction inspired by the Chris Van Allsburg classic. Blackstone Valley is a great place to visit year-round.

## Block Island

Block Island, an 11-square-mile seaside resort located 12 miles off the Rhode Island coast, has been heralded as "One of the Last Twelve Great Places in the Western

Hemisphere." Its rolling green hills and dramatic bluffs are reminiscent of Ireland, while its beautifully restored Victorian hotels and inns preserve the elegance of a bygone era.

The island's 17 miles of pristine, free public beaches are the main attraction of this tiny island, whose people are strongly devoted to preserving the ecology of their home. Block Island conservation groups operate a large trail system on the island, offering walking and hiking paths through grassy meadows, quiet woods and along the sandy shore.

Shops and restaurants are abundant in bustling Old Harbor, which is served by frequent ferry boats from Point Judith, RI. An hour-long ferry ride is the most popular method of traveling to the island, although some prefer to take the easy 20-minute flight from the state airport at Westerly, RI. Ferries also depart, in season, from New London, Conn., Montauk, NY and Newport, RI.

Block Island is close to home but a world away.

## Newport & Bristol County

For more than 375 years, Newport has been welcoming visitors from near and far, which is how this charming coastal enclave earned its moniker "America's First Resort." Perhaps best known as a Gilded Age blue blood playground with legendary lavish mansions, today Newport and its surrounding coastal communities is also a destination for seekers of art and culture, rich history, unspoiled beaches, miles of scenic trails, distinctive shops, critically acclaimed restaurants, one-of-a-kind accommodations, and world-class events.

Barrington, Bristol, Jamestown, Little Compton, Middletown, Newport, Portsmouth, Tiverton and

Warren are equally unique and boast remarkable histories all surrounded by quintessential, small town New England charm. From the spectacular sun-filled days of summer and the majestic colors and crisp salty breezes of autumn, to the serenity of winter and the reawakening season of spring, Newport retains a vibrancy that is palpable all year long.

Choose your own adventure. Explore spectacular Newport Harbor and discover why this special place is known as the "Sailing Capital of the World," trace the ocean's edge with a stroll along legendary Cliff Walk, step back into history by experiencing the famed mansions, savor local flavor at area wineries, indulge in the seasonal menus crafted by award-winning chefs highlighting the harvests of local farmers and fishermen, ride the waves, sink your toes in the sand, be pampered at a luxurious spa or saunter along the bustling downtown waterfront. You can do it all here.

## South County

Experience South County's good nature, where you are invited to unplug and unwind, South County style. Make 20 unspoiled sandy beaches your backyard vacationland, with a South County sunrise being your only wake-up call.

Smell the salt air along miles of sandy shoreline with small town charm complete with iconic boardwalks. Explore the breathtaking beaches of Narragansett, Charlestown and more, including R.I.'s largest beach, Misquamicut, in Westerly. From Wakefield to Watch Hill, taste savory cuisine, shop unique boutiques and feel lively rhythms. Explore 29 forests and wildlife preserves throughout the region offering unspoiled nature walks and wilderness trails. How about an excursion? Paddle through scenic inland waterways that spill directly into the Atlantic Ocean.

South County's many festivals will entice you. Summer's biggest hit besides relaxing at the beach is moving to the music industry's biggest acts at the Rhythm & Roots Festival. Attend the Blessing of the Fleet Festival, where historic maritime traditions take center stage. Fall is all about watching from migrating birds, to the riot of foliage bursting forward, to seals sunning on or off shore the choice is yours. The Annual Cowboy Rendezvous is action filled and promises a galloping good time. Celebrating the holiday season with joyful exhibits at historic seaside villages aglow with luminaria sets the stage for warming up with our art scene. Spring is prime for outdoor recreation be that strolling through the blooms of Dr. Kenney's Azalea Garden or trekking one of our unspoiled scenic management areas or fishing along one of our many waterways.

No matter what the season or activity, now is a great time to visit South County.

## Warwick

Stay in Warwick, see Rhode Island!

Warwick offers a variety of 16 hotels to choose from, amenities galore and its convenient location in the center of RI, makes it the perfect choice for your leisure or business travel needs.

Enjoy dining by the fireside in a historical setting, traditional New England seafood with a waterfront backdrop or good old-fashioned family dining; the choice is yours. If you love live entertainment, Ocean State Theatre, beginning its third successful year, continues to receive rave reviews for its memorable productions including everything from musicals, to comedy and drama. The Theatre offers comfortable seating (not a bad seat in the house), on-site parking and easy access from Route 95. Hint, inquire about Cabaret.

When it comes to shopping, Route 2 in Warwick is the premier shopping destination in Rhode Island, and home to more than 5 miles of retail, restaurants and two indoor malls. Additionally, within the shopping district you will find family fun activities including a trampoline park, ice skating, horseback riding, movie theaters and more.

Now, if the great outdoors beckons you, head over to Harbor Lights, the Valley Country Club or Goddard Park for a round of golf. Explore our 39 miles of coastline that includes breathtaking views from Rocky Point, Conimicut Point right through to Goddard Memorial Park, where you can see the coast via horseback.

Be sure you book an extra night or two because you still have the rest of Rhode Island to experience.

# Historic Providence

## Historic Attractions

Providence experienced sustained periods of economic success early in its history. This, combined with a rich legacy of preservation, has led to a wealth of of well-preserved American architecture and landmarks. Today, many of Providence's historic landmarks are open to the public, including the RISD Museum, the state's leading museum of art and design; the John Brown House Museum, a landmark from the 18th century; and the Governor Henry Lippitt House Museum, an American National Historic Landmark.

## Providence History

Providence was founded in 1636 by renegade preacher Roger Williams, who was forced to flee Massachusetts because of religious persecution. Williams purchased land from the Narragansett Indians and started a new settlement with a policy of religious and political freedom. He named his new home "Providence," in thanks to God for protecting him during his exile from Massachusetts.

Easily accessible by water, Providence became a major New World seaport. During the Revolutionary War, Providence's craftspeople and merchants supplied goods to the Continental and French armies. Ever the entrepreneurs, Providence businesses were financing expeditions to the Mediterranean, Middle East and Far East by 1781. With trade booming, the city grew and flourished. Traditional wooden homes began yielding to ornate brick mansions and citizens constructed elaborate testaments to business, government, and learning. Many of these, like the Rhode Island State House and the Providence Public Library, can be toured today.

The Great New England Hurricane of 1938 wove a path of death and destruction through the city, with a tidalwave like storm surge and wind gusts of more than 100 miles per hour. The storm's effect on Rhode Island was so severe that earthquake instruments 3,000 miles away recorded it on seismographs. In 1954, Hurricane Carol caught Rhode Island by surprise and Providence suffered a great amount of concentrated damage - upwards of $41 million. Gusts of wind, at a rate of 72 to 100 miles per hour, blew into Providence, while portions of the downtown area sat under eight feet of water.

In the late 1970s, the City began to upgrade the infrastructure of the neighborhoods, downtown and commercial districts. For decades, the world's widest bridge had obscured the Moshassuck and Woonasquatucket Rivers, two narrow, but significant waterways which snake through the city of Providence and converge to become the Providence River, the head of Narragansett Bay. In the 1990s, the two rivers running through downtown were uncovered and moved.

Today, those two rivers are edged by cobblestone walkways, flanked by park benches, trees and flowering plants, and bisected by a series of graceful Venetian bridges connecting downtown Providence to the city's East Side. In keeping with this old-world flair, visitors may glide lazily through the waterways in one of the city's gilded gondolas. The centerpiece of this revitalization is WaterPlace Park, which boasts a stone-stepped amphitheater for summer concerts and serves as the starting point for Providence's world-renowned WaterFire, a multi-sensory art installation of nearly 100 dancing bonfires that wind along the Providence River.

Providence also boasts a flourishing cultural and academic community. The Tony Award-winning Trinity Repertory Company and the Providence Performing Arts Center are not only historic landmarks, but also feature Broadway musicals, children's performances, popular seasonal ballets, opera, plays and musical concerts. Students and alumni of Brown University, Providence College and Rhode Island College bring vitality to the city's intellectual life. The famous Rhode Island School of Design lends the city a hipster cool, with many young artists coming to study and staying to begin their careers. The world's largest culinary educator, Johnson & Wales University, has had a tremendous impact on Providence's much-lauded restaurant scene.

## H.P. Lovecraft

Howard Phillips "H.P." Lovecraft, largely considered the father of supernatural horror fiction, was born and lived the majority of his life on the East Side of Providence. In his macabre writing, Lovecraft weaves together what NecronomiCon Providence director Niels Hobbs calls, "A unique blend of cosmic horror and science fantasy known as weird fiction." Lovecraft's writing spanned poetry, letter writing, journalism and most notably fiction, and his style has been emulated by many. His writings serve as inspiration for countless others, including author Stephen King and filmmaker Guillermo del Toro.

NecronomiCon Providence gathers H.P. Lovecraft fans together biennially, with the author's home city of Providence serving as the backdrop. This year's event runs from August 17-20, 2017. There is a city walking tour of sites where Lovecraft spent his time, such as the First Baptist Church in America and the Ladd Observatory. The tour also weaves in historic details within the context of Lovecraft's life. One stop on the tour includes a visit to the John Hay Library where the H.P. Lovecraft Memorial Plaque reads:

*I never can be tied to raw, new things,*
*For I first saw the light in an old town,*

*Where from my window huddled roofs sloped down
To a quaint harbour rich with visionings.*

*Streets with carved doorways where the sunset beams
Flooded old fanlights and small window-panes,
And Georgian steeples topped with gilded vanes-
These were the sights that shaped my childhood dreams.*
*(Sonnett XXX, Background, of Funghi from Yuggoth)*

The Lovecraft Arts & Sciences Council a Providence-based nonprofit education corporation, brings NecronomiCon to Providence as a celebration of the weird fiction written by Lovecraft and authors of a similar vein. NecronomiCon gathers together scholars, authors and fans in an exploration of the literary word and physical place of H.P. Lovecraft. Events commence on Lovecraft's birthday, August 20, and include tours, author readings, film screenings, academic talks, panel discussions, and Lovecraftian gaming, along with Providence-based events such as WaterFire. Intriguing and chilling, Lovecraft and NecronomiCon have built somewhat of a cult following and Providence welcomes fans and followers to share in the curiosity.

## Self-Guided Historic Walking Tours

Submerge yourself in Providence's fascinating history, local lore and quirky tales by taking a self-guided walking tour. Explore the historic east side, the rich culture of the west side or the reinvention of downtown.

Downtown Historic Tour

**This walking tour is self-guided.**
The geographical, political, economic and cultural core of Rhode Island's capital, Providence's downtown neighborhood is bordered by the Providence River and Interstate 95. Colonial Providence was born on the East

Side along the Providence River, but with both the success of the mercantile trade and the industrial revolution, the small city expanded west. Providence became a bustling manufacturing town and by the late 19th century, the city was the transportation hub of southeastern New England due to the extensive railroad network.

The 20th century was an era that started with optimism, followed by the harsh reality of the depression and, ultimately, a transition for downtown. This era also saw the creation of Providence's modern skyline with new Art Deco structures, now icons of the this prosperous time in Providence's history.

Today, downtown Providence is a vibrant mix of nationally recognized arts and cultural institutions, top-ranked restaurants, world-renowned universities, creative industries, financial and legal firms, and locally owned businesses earning the city the name, "The

Creative Capital." Preservation and an appreciation for architecture and history are a constant thread in this neighborhood's story.

## The East Side Historic Walking Tour
This walking tour is self-guided.
A Story of Innovators, Industrialists, Intellectuals and the Irrepressible

Providence is and always was a place for the fiercely independent. The visionary leader Roger Williams established the city in 1636 as a haven for freedom of conscience, where all people could practice their own religious beliefs, a place where they were not merely tolerated, but enjoyed the right of true equality. Freedom of thought reigned, which opened the way for freedom of action.

The economy boomed as the city grew into a great seaport in the 18th century and an industrial powerhouse in the 19th and early 20th centuries. Leading schools, libraries, art clubs and literary societies were established and the arts flourished. But boom times were followed by economic and social busts.

## Providence Personalities: The East Side
### Roger Williams
(1603-1683)

Visionary thinker on religious freedom, equal treatment of Native Americans, and founder of Providence. William's ideas of liberty and freedom of conscience made Rhode Island a haven for persecuted religious groups and laid the groundwork for the ideas of liberty, equality, and the separation of church and state in the U.S. Constitution. He wrote, "**... that no civil** magistrate, no King ... have any power over the souls or consciences of their subjects, in the matters of God ..."

This is the story of the founder of Rhode Island, the first secular State. More than 300 years ago this fiery Christian preacher believed that the wall of separation between Church and State was essential for all other liberties. His ideals, incorporated into the Rhode Island Charter of 1663, laid the foundation for the laws that Thomas Jefferson and James Madison would eloquently affirm in this nation's defining documents: the Declaration of Independence and the Constitution of the United States.

This fiery Christian preacher's name is Roger Williams. The Roger Williams National Memorial and this website are dedicated to his life, legacy, and the ideals we continue to passionately debate today.

## The Brown Brothers

Among the original settlers of Providence in the 1600s, the Brown family emerged as powerful financial, industrial and cultural leaders shaping many of the city's institutions through the centuries, from churches and schools to industry and historic preservation.

**Moses:** (1738-1836) Founder of the first abolitionist society in Rhode Island, Moses Brown was a philanthropist and pioneer industrialist.

**John:** (1736-1803) First from Rhode Island to enter the China Trade, John Brown was founder of the Providence Bank the first bank in Rhode Island, industrialist, U.S. Congressman, and slave trader. He built the grandest house in town and entertained presidents.

**Nicholas:** (1729-1791) Nicholas Brown was a merchant and builder of a great fortune, and was instrumental in relocating Rhode Island College, later named Brown University, to Providence.

**Joseph:** (1733-1785) College professor, Joseph Brown was an astronomer and architect of several of the city's major 18th century landmark buildings.

### William J. Brown
(1814-1885)

The son of slaves owned by Moses Brown, William was a free African American born in Providence. A sailor, homemaker, and temperance movement supporter, Brown wrote in his autobiography entitled Life (1883):

*"Mr. Brown, my grandfather's master, seemed well satisfied with his help and thought that although "hey were his property ... (it was) hence wrong to confine them any longer to servitude ... This was some time before the general emancipation in the State."*

### Matilda Sissieretta Jones
(1868-1933)

Born in Virginia, but later making College Hill in Providence her home, this world renowned soprano sang for four presidents at the White House and the British Royal Family. She was the first African American to perform at the New York City Music Hall, later known as Carnegie Hall.

## Margaret Bingham Stillwell
(1887-1984)

A resident of Benefit Street and the accomplished librarian of
the Annmary Brown Memorial, Margaret Stillwell wrote two
books defending the street's reputation in the 1940s when
the area was in serious decline, calling for residents to repair buildings to "the spirit of youth which ... is still not too far gone to be recaptured." Her vision was realized ten years later when Antoinette Downing and John Nicholas Brown helped launch the Providence Preservation Society.

Margaret Bingham Stillwell (1887-1984), librarian of the Annmary Brown Memorial, was born in Providence on January 26, 1887. She resided on Benefit Street and entered the Women's College in 1905. While she was still a student, she was chosen as an assistant by George Parker Winship, librarian of the John Carter Brown Library, which had recently been located on the Brown campus. She graduated in 1909, and was editor of *Brun Mael,* the Women's College yearbook which appeared for the first time in that year.

She continued her work at the John Carter Brown Library until 1914, when she left for the New York Public Library, where she was a cataloger in the rare book division until 1917. From 1917 to 1953 she was curator of the Annmary Brown Memorial Library, while it was a private library and after it was deeded to Brown in 1948, at which time she joined the University staff as a full professor. Her many publications included

*Incunabula and Americana, 1450-1800, A Key to Bibliographic Study* in 1931, and *Incunabula in American Libraries,*

*A Second Census.* She also wrote a book of verse, *Noah's Ark in Early Woodcuts and Modern Rhyme,* in 1942. The next year she wrote and illustrated *While Benefit Street was Young,* a book intended to defend the street of her childhood from a reputation of sordidness and disrepair suggested by David DeJong's novel, *Benefit Street.* She called on the present residents to repair and paint their houses to carry on "the spirit of youth which ... is still not too far gone to be recaptured." She continued her campaign with the publication in 1945 of *The Pageant of Benefit Street.* She was the first honorary woman member of the Grolier Club, elected in January 1977. She died on April 22, 1984.

## H.P. Lovecraft

(1890-1937)

A master of weird fiction, the East Side resident Lovecraft achieved fame after his death. Author Stephen King described him as "... the 20th century's greatest practitioner of the classic horror tale."

Influenced by Poe, who spent time at the Providence Athenaeum, Lovecraft created a unique world of fantasy and the macabre in stories such as the "Cthulhu Mythos."

In his book "The Shunned House" (1924), inspired by a Colonial house on Benefit Street, his fascination for tombs is apparent.

## Antoinette Forrester Downing

(1905-2001)

Referred to as the matriarch of Providence preservation, Antoinette Downing championed the rescue and restoration of hundreds of 18th and 19th century buildings in the College Hill District. Her visionary work and tireless advocacy in the face of resistance helped save the architectural heritage of the city.

"The city planners are now saying nice things about little old ladies in tennis shoes." - Downing, New York Times, May 2, 1985

## The West Side Historic Walking Tour

This walking tour is self-guided.

**Stories of Immigration and Activism in a Global Neighborhood**

Beyond Interstate 95 lies Providence's West Side. A bridge arching over the interstate takes you into the city of immigrants and strivers, of industrialists in Broadway mansions and mill workers in cramped triple-deckers.

The Colonial town, built on shipping and the slave trade, huddled along the Providence River. By the early 19th century, textile mills had changed the economy, the result of Eli Whitney's cotton gin and Samuel Slater's industrial espionage. The turn of the century saw massive global migrations, and many nationalities contributed to the life of the multilingual city. Today the West Side is a dynamic community, home to those native-born and immigrant, coming from every corner of our country and our planet to build a better life in Providence.

Walk the West Side and see the city of the Irish famine and French Canadian mill workers, the Italian diaspora and Armenian refuge, and the new city being built in one of the most diverse communities in America.

## Providence Personalities: The West Side

Ebenezer Knight Dexter

(1773–1824)

Ebenezer Knight Dexter was a role model of civic philanthropy, leaving large donations of land to the poor and the public good.

Thomas Wilson Dorr
(1805–1854)

Thomas Wilson Dorr was the scion of an old and wealthy family who fought to expand voting rights and led a failed rebellion in 1842.

James Eddy
(1806–1888)

James Eddy was a wealthy art dealer and radical reformer who built a temple dedicated to his independent-minded religion.

Maritcha Remond Lyons
(1848–1929)

Maritcha Remond Lyons testified before the Rhode Island General Assembly at the age of 16 to end public school segregation in Providence and became the first African-American to graduate from Providence High School.

Sarah J. Eddy
(1851–1945)

Sarah J. Eddy was James Eddy's daughter and a radical in her own right, fighting for women's suffrage, social justice, and the humane treatment of animals, as well as being an accomplished artist and photographer.

Anna Garlin Spencer
(1851–1931)

Anna Garlin Spencer was the first female ordained minister in Rhode Island, a journalist, and a leader in social work, social justice and equality.

Luigi Nimini

(1868–1912)

Luigi Nimini was a Verona-born labor organizer, newspaper publisher, and activist for the rights of the poor and working class.

The Tirocchi Sisters

Anna (1884–1947) & Laura (1891–1982)

The Tirocchi Sisters immigrated from Italy and dressed the elite of Providence in Paris-inspired couture for more than 40 years.

Raymond L.S. Patriarca

(1908–1984)

Raymond L.S. Patriarca was the head of one of the most powerful and ruthless organized crime syndicates in the U.S.

## Providence Performing Arts

The theater, Oscar Wilde said, is where we go to get a sense of what it means to be human, because nothing matches the power of a live performance. Providence has long packed a wallop when it comes to the breadth and depth of its performing arts scene.

The Providence Performing Arts Center (PPAC), built in 1928, is a grand architectural gem suitable to the task of hosting the world's best performing artists. PPAC offers a full roster of Broadway shows, concerts, comedians and special performances. Nearby, The VETS hosts an array of performances, from the Philharmonic and ballet to comedians and family shows. This historic theater has been recently restored and upgraded.

From "Julius Caesar" to "A Christmas Carol," Trinity Repertory Company has fed hungry appetites for the dramatic since its founding in 1963. Featuring both local and national talent, Trinity Rep offers classics, world premieres and everything in between during each thoughtfully-crafted season. In the summertime, South County's Theatre-By-The-Sea fills the theatrical void with comedies, musicals and dramas.

Festival Ballet Providence is the state's resident ballet company. Its classically trained, professional ballet dancers perform a wide range of works at three venues: PPAC, The VETS and its own Black Box Theatre on Providence's East Side. Opera Providence offers performances by local and national talent at a variety of locations both indoor and out.

For something a bit eclectic, AS220 provides plenty of inspiration and entertainment as an un-juried and uncensored platform for artists to perform and share their work. AS220 is perhaps best known for its annual outdoor "Foo Fest," a celebration of the arts that strikes at all the senses.

## Live Music in Providence

The Creative Capital is flush with venues to suit all kinds of tastes when it comes to live music. The city that catapulted the Talking Heads to fame after the members of the iconic band went to RISD in the 1970s, and ushered Deer Tick to David Letterman's show decades later, has a great ear. You just have to know where to go.

AS220 and the Columbus Theatre are two key choices at opposite ends of the spectrum. Expect the unexpected at AS220, a local arts force that provides a venue for new and aspiring talent playing everything you can imagine, from punk to blues. They also feature live Irish music at their bar in Downcity on Saturday afternoons. On the West Side, the Columbus Theatre is a haven for local and national musicians and it has garnered accolades such as "Best Folk Venue" and "Best New Music Hot Spot."

Lupo's and its sister property, The Met both legends of the area's music scene still provide an outlet to young and old fans who love live music. Some weekends teenagers flood either dark, no-frills club to hear up-and-coming bands, while on others their parents' generation gets to catch a musician that takes them back to their own salad days.

Restaurants throughout the city also offer rotating performances on an occasional or regular basis. The Dorrance often offers jazz, blues or artists playing the Great American Songbook on weekends in a grand formal setting. Local 121 features Wednesday and Thursday night pianists in their subterranean lounge, which was a legit speakeasy back in the days of prohibition.

## Arts & Culture

Arts & Culture in Providence

Providence was founded by Roger Williams an outcast, a rebel, a creative thinker who dared defy the rules and define his destiny. No wonder then, almost 400 years later, his city of Providence continues to comfort and contain writers, painters, musicians, sculptors, dancers, architects, fashion and jewelry designers indeed those who, like Williams, dance to the beat of their own drum. The Creative Capital has ample opportunity to be inspired by the likes of them all, whatever your taste.

Providence's most significant contribution to the modern artistic world is WaterFire, an installation designed 25 years ago by artist Barnaby Evans. Bonfires in the middle of the river, surrounded by music, performers, food and people, is what Evans envisioned, and on select nights almost year-round, this iconic event delights and enraptures. The works of Evans' less literal compadres those who took to canvas and clay practically watch over this event from the perch that is the RISD Museum. This top design school's museum houses everything from ancient artifacts to contemporary works, and features plenty to see by the most notable masters of the art world. Less notable, but as enchanting, are the works of local and national artists shown in galleries throughout city, including Gallery Z on historic Federal Hill. Gallery Z and others can be visited, via trolley, during popular Gallery Night tours.

On any given night in Providence you are likely to find a well-known Broadway show, a play, or concert at the city's culture homes Providence Performing Arts Center, The VETS, Trinity Repertory Company or the Columbus Theatre each a work of art in their own right. But should you choose to step a bit off the beaten path, you'll make unique and memorable finds, such as the Big Nazo Lab, where ugly-but-lovable life-size monsters come to life. Wherever you choose to go, you'll agree that Roger Williams would be proud.

# Free Events & Attractions

## Children's Museum

Providence Children's Museum, Rhode Island's only hands-on museum especially for children and their families, inspires learning through active play and exploration. The Museum presents interactive exhibits and hands-on programs that explore the arts, culture, history and science and embrace a wide range of learning styles and forms of expression.

## Risd Museum

With a collection of more than 100,000 objects -- ranging from ancient times to the present -- the RISD Museum is a dynamic cultural center offering critically acclaimed exhibitions, lively public programs for all ages, and a renowned museum store, RISD WORKS.

## Museum of Natural History and Planetarium

The Museum of Natural History is Rhode Island's only natural history museum and is home to the state's only public planetarium. For more than a century the museum has served as a unique educational, scientific and cultural resource by offering exciting exhibitions and programming that provide ways for children and families to learn about our world and its people.

## The Stephen Hopkins House (Ca. 1708)

Take a tour of the 1707 home of Declaration-signer Stephen Hopkins, his family and their slaves, eight rooms full of antiques, Hopkins heirlooms and 18th century atmosphere. Learn about Rhode Island's own Founding Father and his house, the city's oldest, moved twice but virtually unmodernized, where George Washington was a guest in 1776. Relax in our parterre garden designed by Alden Hopkins of Williamsburg. We're on Benefit Street between the John Brown House and Roger Williams' First Baptist

Church, a block from the RISD Museum, the Athenaeum, the Brown University campus and Providence's spectacular WaterFire. Open late for full WaterFire lightings, last tour starts at 9:30 p.m.

## Rhode Island State House

The State House is the active seat of Rhode Island's government, but there's more than governing going on in these halls. The impressive building was designed by architectural firm McKim, Mead and White, which also designed many of the Newport Mansions. Visiting the State House is free. Open Monday - Friday (closed on holidays. Free one hour tours every hour from 9 a.m. - 2 p.m. Self-guided tours from the library are until 3:30 p.m

## Providence Athenaeum

The Athenaeum is a unique, independent, member-supported library and cultural center open to the public. Located off of historic Benefit Street, the library offers varied public programming for all ages, which enriches the educational and cultural pursuits of the community. The Athenaeum is free to visit and admission to its programs is free.

# Family Fun

Head to Providence and explore one of the nation's best zoos, let imaginations run wild at the children's museum, or ice skate in the center of downtown Providence. Check out some highlights below and view some other fun things to do in Providence.

### Providence Bruins

The Providence Bruins play at the Dunkin' Donuts Center and are the American Hockey League affiliate of the NHL's Boston Bruins. The P-Bruins offer many special discounted ticket offers and feature giveaway nights including hats, Dunkin' Donuts Mugs, plush

Snoopys and more. For ticket information please visit providencebruins.com or call 401-273-5000.

## Alex and Ani City Center

The ALEX AND ANI City Center provides outdoor ice skating for adults and children plus a Subway concession area rink-side. The ALEX AND ANI City Center is available in the winter for private events on full ice, corporate and social outings, school groups, and in the summer as an event center. For all details about the winter ice skating season and the summer event center season, visit our website at www.providencerink.com or call 401.331.5544.

## Roger Williams Park Zoo

Dubbed "the finest zoo in New England" by the Boston Globe. Walk through this beautifully landscaped 40-acre zoo – one of the nation's oldest – and encounter an African elephant, a Masai giraffe, zebras, a red panda, snow leopard, moon bears, a gibbon, giant ant eater and more in naturalistic settings. Open 10 a.m. to 5 p.m. April - September and 10 a.m. - 4 p.m. October - March with last admission one half hour before closing. Closed Thanksgiving, Christmas and Christmas Eve. Check our website for any additional early closings. The nationally acclaimed Jack-O-Lantern Spectacular runs evenings during October; check website for dates and details.

## Shopping

From boutiques to department stores, Providence and the surrounding areas offer ample shopping. Connected to the Rhode Island Convention Center and the Omni Providence, Providence Place offers visitors a mall with more than 170 shopping, dining and entertainment options. Funky urban chic can be found at one of the many boutiques on Thayer and Wickenden streets, both on the city's tony East Side. From the hip downtown neighborhood, to elegant

Wayland Square and eclectic Federal Hill, there is lots to see and buy. And for those looking to make something old, new again, Providence offers a fun and eclectic vintage retail scene

## Vintage Providence

### Your Guide to Providence Vintage

Experience the hippest, most on-trend, affordable and fun selection of vintage and antique retailers, restaurants, entertainers and service providers in Providence. Click here for the pdf version of the map.

Most businesses are within a 2-mile radius of downtown Providence, while additional listed locations are all within 5 miles of the city. This is a perfect guide to experience the vintage scene in Providence, from shopping to dining, and everything in between. Indulge in the antique and vintage hub of New England - Providence, RI.

## Spas & Salons in The Providence Area

Some Rhode Island hotels offer soothing spas that provide a much-needed oasis from life's daily stresses.

The Spa at the Providence Biltmore (Biltmore Hotel, 11 Dorrance St., Providence, RI) offers services and packages tailored to every potential spa customer, including wedding parties, mothers-to-be, teens, and even the man who has been introduced to the power of pampering. Favorites include: the Island Bliss Pedicure, which includes coconut oils and pure cane sugar; the Beaute Neuve facial, which uses fruit acids and Vitamin C; and the spa's Signature Massage, which spotlights areas aching for attention. Those in need of a serious respite can indulge in a full-day package, including "Rescue Me," which is an 80-minute hot stone massage, hydrating treatment, 50-minute facial, manicure and pedicure.

The G Salon & Spa (Providence Marriott Downtown, 1 Orms St., Providence, RI) boasts a talented staff with extensive experience in hair care and esthetics. Customers can take their relaxation to a new level, by sipping a beer or wine during some treatments. Services run from the traditional - such as massages, manicures and pedicures - to the cutting edge, like eyebrow threading, Keratin treatments and creative "fantasy" makeup.

Nearby Newport's Seawater Spa (Gurney's Newport Resort & Marina, One Goat Island, Newport, RI) offers a tranquil island retreat within Rhode Island's borders. With floor-to-ceiling views of the surrounding sea, Seawater Spa is imbued with the healing power of water.

## Providence Nightlife

There is always something fun and exciting to do in Providence at night. Sing your heart out at karaoke or show off your trivia smarts at one of WRIK Entertainment's events, laugh the night away at the Comedy Connection of Rhode Island, break out some dance moves or sit back and take in the diverse music scene, or tuck away in a corner at one of the many unique bars and lounges. Providence's nightlife scene will make for an amazing and memorable evening in the city

## LGBT Providence

Providence was founded in 1636 by Roger Williams, who believed in tolerance, liberty and free will. That spirit is alive today in bustling, dynamic Providence. Home to seven colleges and universities, the city boasts an eclectic arts scene, critically acclaimed restaurants and a youthful energy.

There is no "gay-borhood" in Providence. Members of the gay and lesbian community can be found throughout the city's many neighborhoods. From Federal Hill Providence's famed Little Italy to the funky cool of the East Side, the city offers plenty to see and do.

# Colleges & Universities

Providence is known as an epicenter of higher education, with eight college and university campuses located in the city. This concentration of faculty and students adds energy to the city and makes an enduring impact on the creative and intellectual landscape of the community.

**Brown University**
Stephen Robert '62 Campus Center
75 Waterman Street
Providence, RI 02912

401-863-1000

www.brown.edu

Brown University is a leading Ivy League institution with a distinctive undergraduate academic program, a world-class faculty, outstanding graduate and medical students, and a tradition of innovative and rigorous multidisciplinary study. Founded in 1764 in Warren, RI, Brown moved to Providence's East Side in 1770 and has been a dynamic force in the community ever since. Notable alumni include John F. Kennedy, Jr. and actress Laura Linney.

**Johnson & Wales University**
8 Abbott Park Place
Providence, RI 02903
1-800-DIAL-JWU
www.jwu.edu

Johnson & Wales University (J&W) offers its students a unique blend of hands-on experience and classic academic instruction. The Downcity Campus, in the heart of the downtown area, houses The Hospitality College and the College of Business, while the Harborside Campus, on the edge of the city, is home to the College of Culinary Arts. J&W was founded in 1914 by two women - Gertrude Johnson and Mary Wales - and continues to leave its mark on the city, most notably through its impact on the critically acclaimed restaurant scene. Notable alumni include celebrity chefs Emeril Lagasse and Tyler Florence.

**Providence College**
1 Cunningham Square
Providence, RI 02918
401-865-1000
www.providence.edu

Providence College (PC) is primarily an undergraduate, liberal arts, Catholic institution of higher education. Nationally recognized for its academic programs, PC is also known for its Division I sports program which has included several nationally ranked men's and women's basketball teams. Founded in 1917, PC makes its home in the city's North End. Notable alumni include NBA Hall of Fame Player and Coach Lenny Wilkins and NBC News Correspondent Mike Leonard.

**Rhode Island College**
600 Mount Pleasant Avenue
Providence, RI 02908
401-456-8000
www.ric.edu

Part of Providence's Mount Pleasant neighborhood, Rhode Island College (RIC) is a public institution of higher education whose primary mission is to offer a quality, affordable education to all Rhode Islanders. Founded in 1854, RIC offers programs in the liberal arts and sciences and in a variety of professional fields. Its performing arts program is highly regarded and draws large audiences to its theater productions. Notable alumni include award-winning actress Viola Davis and Congressman James Langevin.

**Rhode Island School of Design**
Two College Street
Providence, RI 02903-2784
401-454-6100
www.risd.edu

The Rhode Island School of Design (RISD, pronounce riz-dee) is one of the country's leading visual arts, design, architecture and art education institutions. Founded in 1877, RISD is an eclectic community of artists and designers that includes 2,200 students from around the world, approximately 350 faculty and curators, and 400 staff members. Notable alumni include film director Gus Van Sant and "Family Guy" creator Seth MacFarlane.

**URI Feinstein Providence Campus**

80 Washington Street

Providence, RI 02903

401-277-5000

www.uri.edu/prov

The University of Rhode Island has a vibrant Providence Campus located in the heart of downtown Providence. The campus houses the College of Continuing Education, which offers nine undergraduate degree and seven graduate level programs, as well as multiple certificate programs. The campus is also home to an award-winning Child Development Center and the Urban Arts and Culture program, which is a member of Gallery Night.

## Local Sports

Providence's sports scene is steeped in tradition - and a fair share of quirkiness. For example, the city was home to two professional sports teams named the Providence Steamroller (early teams in what eventually became the NFL and NBA). The city's former pro baseball team, the Providence Grays, count Hall of Famers Babe Ruth Charles "Old Hoss" Radbourn among its alumni.

Today, you can see legends in the making at the newly refurbished Dunkin' Donuts Center. After extensive renovations, "The Dunk," as it is affectionately called, glistens in downtown Providence, within walking distance from premier dining options and luxurious hotel accommodations. The Dunkin' Donuts Center seats 14,000 and is conveniently connected to the Rhode Island Convention Center, a multi-purpose facility with 120,000 square feet of exhibition space.

The Dunk houses the Providence Bruins of the American Hockey League and the Providence College men's basketball team, a charter member of the Division-I Big East Conference.

Additionally, Brown University plays their exciting Ivy League brand of football and basketball squarely in the heart of the city and the University of Rhode Island campus houses the pristine Ryan Center facility, located in nearby Kingston.

The state boasts 400 miles of gorgeous coastline, making the state perfect for boating and other seaside activities. Nearby Newport is home to a renowned sailing scene, as well as the International Tennis Hall of Fame. In Pawtucket, Rhode Island, the Pawtucket Red Sox (AAA) boast past and future major leaguers at a fraction of big league prices.

Plus, Providence offers quick and easy access to all of New England's professional sports teams. Highway, train, and airport transportation are mere minutes away.

Visiting Gillette Stadium for a Patriots game? Providence offers game-day rail service from downtown Providence directly to the stadium, providing a more convenient and cost-effective alternative to Boston.

## Outdoor Adventures

### Outdoor Providence Adventures

Despite being an urban capital city, Providence boasts an impressive array of green space and recreational opportunities.

Nationally recognized for its outstanding design, Waterplace Park is the focal point of Providence's revitalized downtown. This four-acre urban park surrounding a tidal basin features an amphitheater, landscaped terraces, and boat landings. A series of Venetian bridges connects downtown Providence to the city's historic East Side. From here you can board a river boat or glide in a gondola down Providence's redesigned rivers. Waterplace Park is also the site of special events such as concerts and the acclaimed WaterFire.

Cited by the National Trust for Historic Preservation as one of America's premier urban parks, Roger Williams Park was designed by Horace Cleveland, noted American landscape architect. With more than 430 acres, the park is comprised of waterways, walks, outdoor gardens, a Carousel Village, Museum of Natural History and Planetarium, the magnificent Temple to Music and Roger Williams Park Zoo.

The Carousel Village features a vintage carousel, pony rides, a themed miniature golf course and kiddie go-boats. The Tennis Center has Rhode Island's only clay courts available for public use. The Dalrymple Boathouse has paddleboats and mini-speed boats and the Botanical Center provides an enviable evergreen oasis.

A tiny jewel of a park on Providence's East Side, Prospect Terrace is the burial place of Rhode Island Founder Roger Williams and boasts a nonpareil city view. Located on Congdon Street, the park is also home to an iconic statue of the Roger Williams.

India Point Park is currently transitioning from a neighborhood park to an architectural focal point. An 18-acre city park overlooking Narragansett Bay, the park underwent a fantastic redesign and improvement under the city's I-Way public works project. Bike paths, playgrounds and waterfront views sparkle amidst lush lawns and a new pedestrian bridge. Water lovers can get their sea fix from the Community Boating Center, which offers sailing lessons and recreational boating opportunities.

## Downtown Providence

Downtown Providence is the humming heartbeat of the city. Home to the city's tallest buildings, a wide range of dining and shopping options, and most recently a growing number of residences, downtown Providence has plenty to offer.

Scenically set upon three rivers (the same rivers in which the city was founded in 1636), the downtown area offers a walkable riverfront in a bustling cityscape. A walk along Memorial Boulevard provides an opportunity to chart the city's interesting architecture - and pick out a perfect spot for a WaterFire viewing. The city's redevelopment of the riverfront has served has a model for other cities around the world.

Today, downtown Providence is a flourishing neighborhood. With dining, shopping and accommodations that are both unique and boutique, the city successfully builds upon a reputation as the "Creative Capital."

Preservation efforts and historic tax credits have jump started redevelopment, allowing resourceful reuse of some of the city's most beautiful buildings. In towering and ornate buildings, once home to dry goods and department stores, you can now find residences, restaurants and galleries.

Events and attractions like WaterFire, ice skating, Gallery Night, Movies on the Block, and even bocce, ensure the city's heartbeat stays strong throughout the evening and all four seasons.

For more information on downtown Providence, including special events and parking, we encourage you to visit our friends In Downcity and the Providence Downtown Improvement District.

## Classes in the Providence Area

Locals and visitors alike may enjoy a host of classes, demonstrations and creative explorations in and around Providence. From cooking classes to the art of steelwork, there is so much to see and do in the Creative Capital.

Cooking Classes

### Chef Walter's Cooking School

Chef Walter offers a range of options, including a cooking camp for teens, recreational classes for foodies, team building, bridal showers and special events, and total immersion classes that teach complete culinary techniques for the food industry.

Professor Chef

Ranging from butcherie and charcuterie to themed menu nights including "Cooking with Julia" and "Downton Abbey," these classes include two instructors and a maximum class size of six students. Professor Chef offers group classes and private classes that teach you how to play with your food. Molecular gastronomy and crafting olive oil soap are also among the weekly class offerings in this intimate setting.

**Easy Entertaining**

These demonstration-based cooking classes showcase three different recipes and a sampling of each dish. Classes are focused around seasonally based ingredients and recipes.

**Johnson & Wales University**

The university offers degree programs in arts and sciences, business, hospitality, physician assistant studies and more, but what they're best known for in Providence is their exceptional culinary arts program. Not just for students, locals and visitors alike can sign up and enjoy Chef's Choice an intensive, one-day cooking and learning experience offered in a variety of gastronomical topics.

Various Community Classes & Events

**Providence Public Library**
The Providence Public Library welcomes visitors and community members with a variety of events, including small business workshops, a history book club, computer classes and story time.

Welding

**The Steel Yard**
For those interested in learning blacksmithing or welding, or simply watching a cool demonstration of the craft, The Steel Yard is the place to explore. Public tours, a jewelry camp and open studio time are also offered in this award-winning Providence industrial arts center.

Boating

## Community Boating Center (CBC)

This nonprofit waterfront organization is committed to keeping sailing affordable and accessible, and offers a range of lessons for beginners and novices, including sailing and kayaking. Choose from youth sailing school, youth summer camp and adult classes. Once structured lessons are complete and adults have passed a class, qualified adult members are free to use CBC boats to sail or paddle at their leisure.

Floral Design

## Studio 539

This modern floral studio is known for its elegant arrangements with stunning palettes of color and texture. Studio 539 also hosts design workshops, such as floral arranging and wreath making.

Gardening

## Cluck!

A shop for urban gardeners and agriculturalists, Cluck! offers classes on everything from choosing your flock (of chicks) to proper garden planning. A local feed and garden center, this shop has a gardening library to peruse and garden to wander. While you're there, stop by the coop and visit Cluck's resident feathered friends.

Languages

## Alliance Francaise de Providence

For those looking to learn another language, choose from French, Spanish, Italian and Arabic. Both adults and kids classes are offered. There are also weekly events, including Café Croissant, where conversations are en Français, and a special foreign film viewing series.

Textiles

### Trad Arts Studio

Located in historic **Slater Mill**, the Trad program includes fiber, textile and maker arts. Set in the birthplace of the American textile industry, Trad classes range from hand weaving to chair caning, natural dyeing and knitting.

Writing

### Goat Hill

Goat Hill hosts workshops on all aspects of writing, from starting a short story, to editing and pitching a finished piece. Goat Hill also hosts author events, such as a recent talk with food writers Ruth Reichl and Michael Ruhlman.

## Restaurants

### Providence Restaurant Weeks

Try out new restaurants or visit old favorites during Providence Restaurant Weeks, which runs for two weeks each January and July. Choose from mouthwatering menus at nearly 100 restaurants. Enjoy three-course lunches at $16.95 and three-course dinners at $29.95 or $34.95, as well as two-for-one specials.

And even though this Restaurant Weeks is over you can still enjoy an amazing meal at any one of the great Restaurants in Providence and throughout Rhode Island. Be sure to check back this winter for the return of Providence Restaurant Weeks in January.

**Downtown Providence Restaurants**
The heart of the city, downtown Providence is compact and walkable, with most restaurants, nightlife, attractions, and shopping located within easy walking distance of area hotels. Three rivers flow through the downtown area, providing lovely walking paths. Providence's downtown is a model for the adaptive

reuse of buildings, having preserved much of the stunning architecture of bygone eras.

### Federal Hill/West Side, Providence Restaurants

Providence's Federal Hill neighborhood has been hailed as "One of the Five Best Little Italys in the U.S." by celebrity Chef Mario Batali. And while the city's rich Italian influence clearly still thrives there, Federal Hill's restaurant scene also offers a diverse selection of cuisines including Indian, Asian and Mexican.

### East Side, Providence Restaurants

From the flickering streetlamps that scallop the edges of Benefit Street to the vast and storied halls of Brown University, Providence's early history is lovingly preserved on the East Side. Yet, the neighborhood is also cool and modern, replete with galleries, restaurants and shops that reflect the edgy, hipster vibe of the renowned Rhode Island School of Design (RISD). These institutions of higher learning combine to give the East Side a personality that is all about art and - as we say in these parts - "wicked smaht."

**Warwick, Ri Restaurants**
You'll find a little bit of everything when it comes to Warwick's restaurant scene. The city offers an array of dining options ranging from contemporary cuisine to a taste of Italy. You can even enjoy fresh seafood selections while taking in a waterfront view.

**Other Rhode Island Restaurants**
Restaurants throughout Rhode Island and the surrounding area offer a variety of dining options. Enjoy seafood fresh from local waters, innovative dishes in world-class restaurants or comfort food served in a cozy eatery, all within a short drive

## Seafood in The Ocean State

Nicknamed the "Ocean State," Rhode Island is lucky to have an abundance of fresh seafood and even luckier to have the culinary talent to interpret it in many delicious, flavorful ways. To taste the best of what our Narragansett Bay has to offer, try one of these restaurants.

**Bluefin Grille**
1 Orms St., Providence, RI 02904
401-272-2400

A place to celebrate life's memorable moments, the Bluefin Grille is a hideaway of casual elegance located in the Providence Marriott Downtown. Cuisine is globally inspired, using local ingredients with an emphasis on responsibly caught seafood.

**Finn's Harborside**
38 Water St., East Greenwich, RI 02818
401-884-6363

Previously Harbourside Lobstermania, Finn's Harborside is the pinnacle of seaside dining in East Greenwich. Delivering the most delectable seafood,

Finn's Harborside is here to give you the best taste of Rhode Island.

**Hemenway's**
121 South Main St., Providence, RI 02903
401-351-8570

"Rhode Island's Premier Seafood Address," Hemenway's is Providence's original downtown, riverside restaurant with a national reputation for serving only the freshest seafood while delivering genuine hospitality in a relaxed atmosphere.

**Legal Sea Foods**
2099 Post Rd., Warwick, RI 02886
401-732-3663

The signature dish at Legal Sea Foods - really fresh fish. In the "Ocean State," Legal Sea Foods makes waves serving more than 40 varieties of fish and shellfish throughout the year.

**Lobster Pot**
119 Hope St., Bristol, RI 02809
401-253-9100

Enjoy this classic Rhode Island seafood restaurant located in Bristol. Established in 1929, the Lobster Pot offers cuisine and an atmosphere that complement each other perfectly.

**Matunuck Oyster Bar**
629 Succotash Rd., South Kingstown, RI 02879
401-783-4202

The Matunuck Oyster Bar offers waterfront dining and prides itself in uniting fresh, locally grown produce with locally farm-raised and wild caught seafood to make the freshest dishes you'll find.

**McCormick & Schmick's**

11 Dorrance St., Providence, RI 02903

401-351-4500

McCormick & Schmick's, a casual dining restaurant features more than 30 varieties of fresh seafood and shellfish daily, along with savory steaks, chicken and pasta. Its timeless atmosphere creates an inviting ambience.

**Providence Oyster Bar**
283 Atwells Ave., Providence, RI 02903

401-272-8866

Providence Oyster Bar, the leading seafood restaurant in Providence, exemplifies the freshest in quality seafood, first-class service and atmosphere.

## Other Restaurants That Have Great Seafood Options
**The Capital Grille**

New Providence Travel, Rhode Island

10 Memorial Blvd., Providence, RI 02903
401-521-5600

The Capital Grille boasts an atmosphere of power dining, relaxed elegance and style. The Capital Grille serves classic steakhouse offerings such as chops, large North Atlantic lobsters and fresh seafood. Enjoy an award-winning wine list or their signature "stoli doli" martini.

**Capriccio**
2 Pine St., Providence, RI 02903
401-421-1320

Providence's famed mecca for sophisticated European dining, where both locals and out-of-towners are deliciously pampered. Enjoy the European twist on the seafood dishes offered at Capriccio along with the perfect glass of wine.

**DeWolf Tavern**

259 Thames St., Bristol, RI 02809

401-254-2005

Located in Bristol, DeWolf Tavern serves contemporary American cuisine on the bay. Enjoy a breeze off the ocean while enjoying a fresh fish choice off the raw bar menu and your choice of a fine wine to sip while you watch a perfect sunset.

**Mill's Tavern**
101 North Main St., Providence, RI 02903

401-272-3331

Winner of the 2015 OpenTable Diners' Choice Award, Mill's Tavern is a small, chic restaurant located in downtown Providence. Visit Mill's Tavern to experience an array of "Raw Bar" choices off their menu.

**Ten Prime Steak & Sushi**

55 Pine St., Providence, RI 02903

401-453-2333

Dine in a modern metropolitan eatery in the heart of historic downtown Providence. Ten strives to deliver the best cuts of some of the most award-winning steaks and the freshest sushi in Rhode Island.

## Providence Burgers

Providence was recently named one of the five best cities for burgers by Travel Pulse ... and boy do we have some good burger spots. Burgers come in many variations including veggie, turkey or bison, and Providence has it all. Grab a craft beer while you are in town to compliment your amazing burger at one of our many pubs and brew houses. Take a look at some of the local spots and specials.

**GPub**

61 Orange St., Providence, RI 02903
401-632-4782

Located on the ground floor of the ProvidenceG, GPub's eclectic menu and American industrial atmosphere make it the perfect place to stop in for a quick lunch or a burger and a beer. Try one of their pre-designed burgers or create your own with an array of topping options.

**Harry's Bar & Burger**
121 North Main St., Providence, RI 02903
401-228-7437

Harry's Bar & Burger, a "Fast Slow Food" establishment, specializes in burgers and always keeps in mind their fresh ingredients mission. Choose from one of their many specially designed burgers. Enjoy half-priced burgers daily from 3 p.m. to 5 p.m. #1 Burger - CNN

**Luxe Burger Bar**
5 Memorial Blvd., Providence, RI 02903

401-621-LUXE

Located in the heart of Downtown Providence, Luxe Burger Bar allows you to build your own burger, ranging from beef, turkey and chicken, to bison, tuna and vegan. With its trendy atmosphere, Luxe is the perfect place to grab a burger.

**Rick's Roadhouse**
370 Richmond St., Providence, RI 02903

401-272-7675

For BBQ right in Providence, Rick's Roadhouse has all of your favorites, including some mouthwatering burgers. Choose from a menu of craft burgers. And don't forget to try a bison burger because only the best BBQs have bison burgers.

# Events

No matter when you plan your visit, you will find something fun to do. From historic tours to WaterFire, performing arts to food festivals, and everything in between, there are events for every season.

The Providence area plays host to a wide range of nightlife events, including karaoke and trivia nights, comedy shows and more. And for those looking for something more food-focused, there are also a variety of dining specials and events.

## Annual Events in Providence

Winter, spring, summer and fall, Rhode Island hosts annual events that are inspiring, iconic and entertaining.

### Providence Restaurant Weeks

One of America's hottest food cities (Travel + Leisure mag's opinion, as well as others'!) must host show-stopping Restaurant Weeks, and Providence does in January and July. You'll be hard-pressed to find a restaurant in the city that doesn't participate with prix-fixe special menus featuring three- and four-course meals and a great price. It's the ideal excuse to try a new place or return to an old favorite.

## Eat Drink RI Festival

Local chefs and the people who love them descend on the city each April for this event, which highlights the Rhode Island food, farm and restaurant scene with lectures, demos and, of course, tastings. The festival is both upscale and casual, paying homage to everything from food trucks (there are dozens of them in Little Rhody) to restaurants and chefs who've garnered national attention.

## WaterFire

This iconic event has helped put Providence on the top destinations map with its installations of bonfires lit along the middle of the city's rivers. Locals and tourists alike come out on certain nights from May through November to revel in the sights, sounds and smells golden embers, mystical music, performing artists and of course, lots of food. Artist Barnaby Evans, who created WaterFire almost 30 years ago, has been internationally recognized for this unique celebration.

## Federal Hill Stroll

One of America's oldest and best Little Italy neighborhood swings open its doors for an evening in June to welcome new customers and say hello to regulars. Buy and wear a button that will allow you access to dozens of restaurants, cafes and shops along Atwells Avenue, and experience Hill hospitality with complimentary samples of food and drink. Stop in DePasquale Square for live music, dancing, and people watching.

## Rhode Island PrideFest and Parade

Providence is proud to be one of the top destinations for LGBT tourists in part because Rhode Island Pride works so hard to advocate for the rights of their community. This annual weekend-long event, held in June, celebrates the culture, art, music and diversity of the local and regional LGBT population with concerts, bar and club events, and a nighttime illuminated parade as colorful and fun as any you've ever seen.

## Festival of Historic Houses
The Providence Preservation Society celebrates the city's gorgeous architectural gems, some dating to the 1600s, with this annual June festival. The tour provides a rare opportunity to step inside historic properties and learn about their origins and inhabitants while viewing firsthand the modern day living spaces indoor and out in these prized, preserved places.

## AS220's Foo Fest

Providence's most unique arts organization, AS220, which provides artists of all kinds space to celebrate their work, seeks with Foo Fest to transform downtown Providence's Empire Street into a spirited block party attracting thousands of revelers. A genre-spanning bill of nearly two-dozen musical acts takes over the indoor and outdoor stages of Foo Fest. The festival also features more than a dozen artist installations and participatory creative activities, including family-friendly offerings.

## Independence Day Celebration

In an invigorating display of patriotism the Rhode Island Philharmonic Summer Pops perform an outdoor concert each July Fourth at India Point Park in Providence. Pull up a blanket on the lawn by the water and enjoy the music, food trucks, street performers and more, and cap it all off with a grand fireworks display.

## Flickers Rhode Island International Film Festival

This week-long August event is the largest public film festival in New England and a qualifying event for the Academy of Motion Pictures Arts & Sciences and the British Academy of Television and Film Arts awards. The festival welcomes entries from Rhode Island and throughout the world and showcases the films, with post-viewing lectures and events, across the city. For film lovers of all kinds, it's a must-see.

## Jack-O-Lantern Spectacular

The wooded walkways and paths of Roger Williams Park Zoo are transformed each October into a spooky and oh-so-cool venue for thousands of illuminated pumpkins. Each jack-o-lantern is artistically and meticulously carved into the likeness of celebrities, scenes and scary Halloween designs. The event is the perfect way to get into the spirit of Halloween and enjoy the autumn harvest.

## Rhode Island Comic Con

This fun three-day event is Rhode Island's premier toy, comic book, media and collectibles event. Held in November, it attracts thousands of eager fans of everything from "Star Trek" to "Star Wars." Dozens of celebrities are featured at meet-and-greet and photo-op events, lectures and parties. Many attendees come in costume, making the people watching spectacular!

## Dining Specials & Events

Amazingly (and deliciously), Rhode Island has about 100 restaurants for every 100,000 residents, making it one of the most densely-populated restaurant states in America. Add two more factors the world-class culinary school at Johnson & Wales University and the wide-range of ethnic cultures and you've got what Travel + Leisure magazine and others have dubbed one of the top foodie destinations in the nation.

One of the best ways to get a feel for the tight-knit chef and food community here is to visit one of the state's many farmers markets. The most popular is the Saturday Hope Street Market, where hundreds of the best farms, chefs and purveyors set up, and the friendly vibe means you can chat, learn and taste along the way. Dozens of other farmers markets occur all over the state, and Farm Fresh Rhode Island's website lists them all.

Another great lay-of-the-land strategy is to sample some of the state's fabulous food trucks. There's more than 60 to choose from and they serve everything epic gourmet grilled cheese, fresh-shucked oysters, Korean barbecue and Mexican street food. Food Truck Friday at Roger Williams Park happens at lunchtime weekly at Carousel Village and features a couple of different choices each week. The Food Truck Marketplace in downtown's Kennedy Plaza hosts a rotating array daily for the lunchtime masses.

Annually, there are lots of fun events and festivals for all to enjoy. Providence Restaurant Weeks takes place each January and July and features three-course, prix fixe menus at nearly 100 restaurants. The EatDrinkRI Festival focuses on local chefs and farms and kicks off festival season each April with four days of tastings and educational events. In June, the Little Italy section of Providence opens its doors for the Federal Hill Stroll, a night where restaurants along Atwells Avenue offer samples of entrees and beverages. The Rhode Island Seafood Festival takes over the city's India Point Park for a weekend each September, and the latest, the Ocean State Oyster Festival, returns in the fall.

# Directions & Parking in Providence

Downtown Providence is conveniently located off of Interstate 95. Travelers looking for assistance in planning their trip are invited to drop by the Visitor Information Center, located on the ground floor of the Rhode Island Convention Center.

**From 95 North**
Take Exit 22A, Downtown Providence. Follow the signs towards Downtown/Convention Center. At the light, turn right onto Francis St. At the next light, turn right onto Sabin St. You will find 15-minute parking available in front of the main entrance of the RI Convention Center.

**From 95 South**
Take Exit 22A, Downtown Providence. Follow the signs towards Downtown/Convention Center. Go through the first light in the right-hand lane. Continue to the second light, take a right onto Exchange Street. At the stop sign, take a right onto Exchange Terrace. Proceed

straight through the next set of lights, bear left at the fork onto Sabin Street where

# Tourist Attractions in Providence

At the northern tip of Narragansett Bay, Rhode Island's capital city is wonderfully compact, diverse, and eccentric. Its long history, from its founding by dissidents escaping Puritan Massachusetts to its colorful contemporary politics, may explain the eccentricities. These combine with its wealth of historic sights (entire neighborhoods are designated historic districts) and artistic highlights to make Providence fun to visit. In addition to offering a number of top tourist attractions, Providence is lively and full of character, a city of distinctive neighborhoods reflecting both its ethnic and cultural diversity. A high-powered student population from Brown University, Rhode Island School of Design (RISD), and Providence College keep it young and vibrant, along with insuring a rich arts and intellectual scene. People here take their restaurants seriously, so be sure and ask locals for dining suggestions - you'll always get an informed opinion.

## WaterFire

At least twice a month between mid-May and late November, braziers in the middle of the river are filled with bonfires that light Downcity Providence. During "Full WaterFire," more than 80 fires blaze from Waterplace Park to Memorial/South Main Street Park. "Basin Fire WaterFire" events are smaller versions lighting 22 braziers in the Waterplace Park Basin and five more toward Providence Place mall. During WaterFire, the four-acre Waterplace Park and Riverwalk become a festival of arts and music as young and old alike enjoy their city's revitalization and cultural vibrancy.

## Benefit Street "Mile of History

On this mile-long street traversing the steep hillside that rises from the river to the Brown University campus, you can see an architectural history of Providence. At one end are the restrained and elegant Federal period homes, beautifully restored with their doorways in a neat row close to the street, and as you walk farther, you'll see grand homes set back on their lawns, and later Victorian, even Arts and Crafts-style residences. Several of the city's attractions are among them - the Governor Stephen Hopkins House with its terraced garden, the Athenaeum (with Edgar Allen Poe connections), and the John Brown House. You can get details on the various buildings from an excellent Benefit Street walking tour booklet from the Providence Preservation Society.

## RISD Museum of Art

Whether your artistic passion is for French Impressionists or Japanese prints, or your design tastes run to ancient Egyptian, early American, or cutting-edge contemporary, you'll find enough to keep you happy in the depth and breadth of this museum's collections. The Rhode Island School of Design (RISD), one of America's top art colleges, reflects its own wide range of specialties in the objects chosen for its museum. Needlework and textiles, sculpture from ancient to Rodin, Asian art, videos, furnished Federal period rooms, and galleries of priceless paintings comprise dozens of individual collections. So many outstanding works are here that each of its separate collections would be enough to make a museum of its own.

## John Brown House

President John Quincy Adams described the 1786 home of merchant John Brown as "the most magnificent and elegant mansion that I have ever seen on this continent." From its lofty hillside setting he could keep an eye on his China Trade ships and warehouses at India Point, the source of his considerable wealth. That he was a man of taste as well as wealth and prominence is clear from the house, with its French wallpapers, finely worked decorative detail and moldings, and original Brown family furniture. For an unparalleled view of 18th-century life for the Providence aristocracy, as well as a look at some of the best pieces by Rhode Island cabinetmakers that you'll find anywhere, don't miss this magnificent home.

## Brown University

The Brown University campus crowns College Hill and has since 1770; its oldest building and still the center of the campus is University Hall, which served as a barracks and hospital during the Revolution. The impressive Van Wickle Gates open only twice a year, on the first day of classes and for the commencement procession in May. Stamp collectors will want to see the complete collection of US postage stamps in the John Hay Library; the John Carter Brown Library has a collection of rare early maps.

The free David Winton Bell Gallery has excellent changing exhibits of contemporary and historic art. For student-led campus tours, visit the Corliss-Brackett House. Here's a secret you probably won't hear about on the tour: Brown's Environmental Center has a conservatory on Waterman Street, a glass house with a jungle of plants and exotic flowers thriving inside through the coldest of winter days. Few know about it, but the center advises that "Artists, gardeners, tinkerers, dreamers, readers, thinkers, general plant lovers, and green and brown thumbs are encouraged to visit."

## Governor Henry Lippitt House

Even in this posh neighborhood of grand old homes, the 1865 mansion of Governor Henry Lippitt stands out. The 30-room Renaissance Revival villa/Italian palazzo is even more impressive inside, where the stenciling, stained and etched glass, and faux wood and marble finishes make it one of New England's finest interiors - arguably the best in terms of Victorian decoration. The ornate woodwork, original family furnishings, and mechanical systems that were revolutionary for the mid-19th-century combine to make it a museum of Victorian interior decoration and a window into the life of a prosperous Victorian family. Generations of the Lippitt family - they were heirs to a RI textile manufacturing fortune - lived in the house for 114 years, and their story comes alive in the excellent guided tours, the only way you can see the exuberant interior.

## Roger Williams Park and Zoo

Roger Williams Park covers 435 acres with gardens, a lake with a 1915 bandstand, an amphitheater, greenhouses, the 1773 Betsy Williams Cottage and a children's area with a carousel, trackless train rides, and other activities. Also in the park is a Museum of Natural History with insects, minerals, fossils, and the state's only planetarium. But what draws most visitors is the 40-acre Roger Williams Park Zoo, one of the oldest zoos in the country, but a paragon of modern zoo design and concept. At this kid-friendly and largely cage-free place you can meet a snow leopard, giraffe, elephant, zebra, wildebeest, alligator, kangaroo, and red panda, and small-fry can climb into the tree house or go for a camel ride. If you don't like the notion of caged animals and want to learn something about them and their habitats instead of just parading past, this is the zoo for you.

## Culinary Arts Museum

If it relates to the history or culture of cooking, eating, or the various culinary industries, this foodie paradise probably has it. Along with permanent displays, multiple special exhibits highlight themes drawn from the museum's collection of more than 250,000 items. Collections include rare cookbooks, the interiors of diners, and an 1833 New Hampshire stagecoach tavern, artifacts from ancient Rome, fast-food wagons, neon signs, kitchens - from open hearth and wood stoves to microwaves, and special exhibits might explore the world of famous chefs, cooking competitions, or dinners served at the White House.

## The Arcade and Downcity

Spared the ravages of urban renewal that robbed so many American cities of their early 20th-century architectural heritage, Providence was too poor to tear down old fashioned commercial blocks of its old downtown (called Downcity here), so instead they "modernized" by covering the facades with wood to imitate the popular bland '70s style. This benign neglect saved what other cities now regret having lost - beautiful and astonishingly well-preserved decorative details and priceless period architecture. Interiors fared well, too, and the magnificent banking halls, many of whose elaborate high ceilings had been covered, are again resplendent and put to new uses.

Amid the Art Deco and Beaux-Arts buildings and late Victorian terracotta facades stands Downcity's icon, The Arcade. Open again and refurbished after a five-year closing, this imposing granite building was America's first shopping mall, built in 1828. After you step inside to browse in its shops - all local businesses -- be sure to look at both its facades. The two owners couldn't agree on the style, so each hired his own architect to design one end. The oldest building in the area, the Beneficent Congregational Church on

Weybosset Street, was built 20 years before The Arcade, although its portico and dome were not added until 1836.

## Federal Hill

Atwells Avenue atop Federal Hill, the hill that rises to the west of Downcity, is the vibrant heart of Providence's large Italian American community. That community now spreads throughout the city, but the concentration of restaurants, cafés, and shops selling Italian foods along Atwells Avenue and its adjacent streets and squares stems from the days when immigrants grouped closely with others who shared their language and traditions. Today, Italian cooks shop in its delis and bakeries to find fresh-made mozzarella, tangy pickled cherry peppers, imported cured meats, and golden panettone. Come here to eat an Italian meal, whether it's spaghetti and red sauce (called simply "gravy" here) in elbow-bumping conviviality or northern Italian dishes served in a linens-and-crystal setting. It's also the place to linger over cappuccino or a dish of gelato at a sidewalk cafe, or join in a boisterous street festival on Columbus Day.

www.ingramcontent.com/pod-product-compliance
Lightning Source LLC
Chambersburg PA
CBHW021113080526
44587CB00010B/498